A Decade of Merriment and Mayhem
in a Town Near Normal

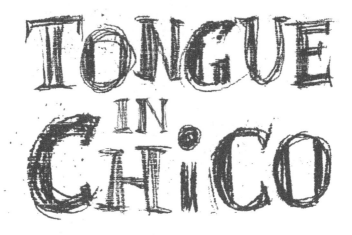

TONGUE IN CHICO

Conceived and written by C L Smith

Designed and illustrated by Randy Nowell

Tenderfoot Books
Sonoma

Tenderfoot Books
May 2021

TONGUE IN CHiCO

Library of Congress Control Number: 2020917441

ISBN	978-1-7356132-0-8	paperback
ISBN	978-1-7356132-1-5	Kindle Edition
ISBN	978-1-7356132-2-2	Audible

Additional copies of this book are available on
Amazon and **Kindle**.
See **www.TongueInChico.com**
for other locations.

Dedicated to my 99-year-old father,
Jasper Eugene Smith,
a decorated World War II US Marine Corps
combat veteran and amazing
father of seven, whose sage wisdom
and advice I obviously ignored.

PART 1

PIONEER Daze in a Town OFF NORMAL

A Day in the Life of a **Chico State Student**

Ten Commandments for **College Students**

How to **Break Up** a Kegger, **DOGGY STYLE**

NAKED Truths about **Skinny-Dipping**

CSU SKINNY DIPPING TEAM

It's Good to be #1!

My father was always dumbfounded when he heard me **bragging** about **Chico State's** reputation as **The #1 Party School in the Nation.**

Of course, we were proud to be at the top of **Playboy** magazine's famous poll for several years in a row. For some reason our parents who were **footing the bill** didn't see it like that.

The Playboy poll put us on the map.
We knew driving in we weren't going to make any **Top 10** university lists with Harvard, Stanford and the like.

So, it was party on, Garth, and there wasn't even a Garth yet.

Like our beloved **Zig-Zags**, the good times rolled pretty much non-stop through the **1970s** in Chico.

My generation and I skipped town just before the wheels fell off the beer cart around 1980.

The time capsules here are from that innocent era before **AIDS**, **Rodney King** and the **crack** epidemic but after **herpes** and **Cracker Jacks**.

Chico's famous
Pioneer Week
had already devolved into
the infamous **Pioneer Daze**
but hadn't crashed into
the party-ending street
riots of the **Pyro Years** yet.

That's when the **Animal House**-emulating
latchkey kids of the early 80s ruined it for everyone.

Meanwhile, my cohorts and I were
already out in the **real world**,
pretending to be adults.

Read Wikipedia for more context.

Better yet, step back in time with
me to that crazy age between the
60s and **80s**...

the rollicking 1970s

...when **skinny-dippers** ruled
Upper Bidwell, the pot grown
in the foothills sold for
$6,000 a pound, and the
mirrors of **Craig Hall** were
lined with pure **cocaine**.

And/or **baby laxative**.

A Chico State
of Mind

In the fall of 1974, I moved from Upper Malibu Shores (aka Ventura) to the quaint Northern California college town of **Chico**, where my "adolescent drivel" quickly caught the imagination of the local literary community.

"Regarding C L Smith's humor, Jesus, what an idiot! It's a slap in the face to productive working people everywhere if he gets paid a penny for this adolescent drivel."

I actually made $150 over three years for writing that "adolescent drivel."

"Once again, we have been subjected to C L Smith's inane perception of Chico lifestyles."

Yikes.

Could I have been this bad?

You be the Judge!

Degrees of
SEPARATION

You might think from reading this book I'm ragging on the education I received at Chico State. You'd be as wrong as a **skinny-dipper in a Brooks Brothers suit**.

I'm not going to say my master's degree in English from Chico led directly to my helping create some of the most loved and hated national TV ads of the 2000s. Or to my co-leading the **North American launch** of **Android** smartphones. Or in 2012 to my being named one of the **nation's top** media executives while managing a stable of ten ad agencies from **Verizon Headquarters** outside New York City

But my five years of **Skoalastic Achievement** and **Sleep-Deprivation** at Chico State sure as **Hell Town** didn't hurt me in the **dog-eat-dog** wireless marketing wars. In fact, that prestigious Chico **pedigree** gave me a **leg up** in one **dog-and-pony** show after another.

Ivy-League Round Pounders

One of the **general managers** who recommended me for a significant promotion looked at my resume and said:

*"Thank God you're a state university guy.
We've got enough **Ivy Leaguers** round-pounding it up at headquarters as it is."*

Another of my senior mentors said:

*"Operationally, I'll take a state U guy any day over some smart-ass think-tanker from Harvard or Stanford.
Half those guys will wind up being
VPs of Looking Out the Window anyway."*

Mount McKinsey

Another market president gave me a heads-up about a bad-ass productivity consultant from **McKinsey**.

"You're from Chico, right? He's from Harvard. Fuck that. He works for you now. Don't let him forget it for a minute."

Turned out the McKinsey consultant was a **great guy** named **Ujjal Kohli**. Wicked smart minus the wicked part.

One of the greatest Chico State success stories ever is a fellow **Chico alum** and former colleague of mine who went **toe-to-toe** with **Steve Jobs**, ruled over more Ivy League MBAs than you can throw an **iPhone** at, and was the **most powerful woman** in wireless for a decade.

This superstar from Chico State is named **Marni Walden**, class of '89. She looks like **Gwyneth Paltrow** and kicked more Ivy League ass than **Teddy Roosevelt**. But that's another story for my next book.

The bottom line to this one is simply:

Don't mess with Chico!

But it's okay to LOL remembering the good times we had. Or wished we had, right. Especially in the midst of a frigging pandemic.

If Covid-19 didn't made you sick, maybe this book will.

Let's give it the old college try and see!

A Day in the Life of a Chico State Student

How does the average Chico State college student spend a typical day? As a four-year veteran and graduate of that **venereal institution**, I've had ample opportunity to study this question, and it looks something like this:

A.M.

10:30 Crawls out of bed, turns on stereo full-blast, wakes everyone within one-block radius.

10:40 Enjoys hearty breakfast of **cornflakes** and **beer**.

11:00 Rides bicycle to school. Rolls through seven stop signs without looking. Hits two **jaywalkers**.

11:15 Bicycle is stolen while showing accident victims his **fake ID** and scribbling out a made-up phone number.

11:22 Watches educational film, Wife Swapping Among Polar Bears, in Modern Mating class.

P.M.

12:10 Skips History of Disco class to play Frisbee.

12:18 Hits passing freshman in **head** with Frisbee.

12:23 Hits passing freshman in **groin** with Frisbee.

12:25 Has Frisbee broken over his head and stuffed into his mouth by angry freshman.

12:30 Assaulted outside the library by **Hare Krishnas**, petition-pushers and a slow streaker.

12:38 Signs petition to let dogs run free on campus as lc as they don't **make any mistakes in the classroom**

12:40 Scrawls **obscene poem** on BMU restroom wall.

12:47 Signs petition to fine dogs for every mess they make in the classroom.

12:52 Steals **Bic pen** from A.S. Bookstore.

12:58 Signs petition to **outlaw petitions**.

1:06 Attacked by hippie giving away **diseased kittens**.

1:30 Applies for **Food Stamps**. Granted $100 worth.

2:05 Stops at dealer's house on way home from Food Stamp office and buys **$100** worth of **cocaine**.

2:30 Picks up faithful childhood pet, a yellow Labrador, at home and returns to campus.

2:35 **Old Yeller** tugs playfully on terrycloth **gym shorts** of attractive coed.

2:45 Yeller gets stuck on a golden retriever while mating **doggie-style** outside **chancellor's office**.

3:00 Skips Dog Obedience class to take exhausted family pet tubing. Too dog-tired to dog-paddle in strong current, **Old Yeller** drowns.

5:30 Returns home to study. Turns stereo on **full blast** and broils a steak instead.

6:35 Forgets about steak and neglects to mute stereo while calling roommate ad for "creek-view home with benefits offered by fun-loving **party girls** seeking **well-endowed males**."

6:37 Fun-loving party girls can't hear a word he's saying, **hang up** on him.

6:55 Sees steak burning, puts out **kitchen fire.**

8:30 **Horny.** Invites girlfriend over.

8:45 Cocaine turns out to be **baby laxative.**

8:48 Clogs **toilet.**

8:50 Girlfriend leaves in a hurry after knocking on bathroom door for two minutes.

9:15 Crams for test in Solo Gratification class.

10:30 Goes to fraternity kegger. Drinks 30 **warm beers** from **plastic red cups**, force-fed **20 goldfish.**

11:35 Stopped by police for driving wrong way on Main Street.

11:40 Arrested for driving under the **influence of goldfish** and **possession of baby laxative.**

A.M.

2:10 Divorced parents, living 300 miles apart in the East Bay and SoCal, agree to split cost of **bail bond.**

2:30 Stumbles home, falls into bed.

9:00 Skips Nuclear Physics For Dummies class.

10:30 Crawls out of bed, turns on stereo full blast, pours **warm beer** on **bowl of cornflakes.**

~ February 9, 1978

Adopt a
College Student!

Won't you complete this simple questionnaire and befriend a needy college student through our Save the College Students Fund? **For only $20 a day**, your money can help a college student buy the **drugs** and **alcohol** he needs to make it through the hot summer ... the **new clothes** she needs for a **fulfilling nightlife** ... the **expensive gasoline** he needs to power his parents' new **ski boat**.

While $20 may not mean much to you, for a **struggling college student**, it can mean the difference between partying every night and having to find a job.

Tell us how you want to help by
answering these questions:

What kind of student would you like to adopt?

☐ Straight ☐ Lesbian

☐ Gay ☐ Undecided

If gay, would you prefer?

☐ Declared ☐ Closet

What kind of picture would you prefer?

This is a difficult choice for some patrons, because so much depends on what the student looks like:

☐ Clothed

☐ Naked ☐ Wait and see

Would you like to exchange correspondence?

If desired, this will help your student mooch more money off you. Since most college students are illiterate, a representative will keep you informed of the fun your student is having.

☐ Yes ☐ No

Would you like weekly progress reports?

These will show how your money is being spent, what kinds of drugs your student is using, preferred sexual positions, number of genuine orgasms experienced and incidence of venereal disease.

☐ Yes   ☐ No

Please check the types of activities you'd like your student to spend your money on, though it's unlikely he or she will pay any attention to your suggestions:

☐ New stereo   ☐ Beer

☐ Movies   ☐ Cocaine

☐ Clothes   ☐ Prostitutes

☐ Concerts   ☐ Water Skiing

☐ Marijuana   ☐ A New Car

☐ All of the Above

(Best Value!)

How do you wish to send your money?

☐ $20 Daily

☐ $140 Weekly

☐ $600 Monthly

Here's What You'll Receive!

✓ A **laminated copy** of your student's arrest record.

✓ A monthly shipment of **beer bottle tops**, empty baggies and **used birth control devices**. All sealed in an attractive carrying case and autographed by your student.

✓ A **Foster Parent Information Kit**, with updates on all the **wholesome fun** your student is having with your money.

✓ At least two **obscene phone** calls threatening you with physical harm if you don't increase your student's monthly support payments.

Won't you get started today and send your first check to:

C L Smith
P.O. Box 69
Chico, CA 95926

~ May 24, 1979

There's
A NEW SHERIFF
in Town

Maybe I'll get to meet him!

The **Day in the Life**
and **Adopt a College Student**
articles put me on the map as a
new literary force to be
reckoned with in Chico.

In the coming weeks, my house
off fraternity row on **Normal Avenue**
would be toilet papered three times.

Oh, the humanity.
Finally, my career was taking off!

Ten Commandments
for
College Students

Kiss up to thy professors.

Thus, they may giveth thou a passing grade even when thou doth not do any homework and flunk all their tests.

Remember thy sabbath, to keep it mellow.

Six days thou shalt party and get drunk.
But on the seventh day, thou shalt stay in bed and recuperate from hangovers.

Thou shalt not commit adultery.

Thou shalt always act like a spoiled brat,
even if thou art approaching 30.

Thou shalt not covet thy neighbor's houseplants.

But thou may covet his stash, stereo, record collection and girlfriend if thou art careful.

Thou shalt not dance on thy kitchen table.

Try thy coffee table first.

Thou shalt not stop at stop signs on thy bicycle.

However, thou mayest take thy
Lord's name in vain if a car runneths over thou.

Thou shalt not sneeze on thy neighbor's cocaine.

For the Lord asks that ye be not wasteful.

Thou shalt take to thine bed a new partner every week.

So that thou may have plenty to brag or gossip to thine roommates about.

Thou shalt blast thine stereo at least 10 hours a day.

The Lord recommendeth Black Sabbath.

Thou shalt learn to count to ten.

So that thou can see this list only goes to nine.

~ March 8, 1979

New Year's Resolution

I will not pick up a free kitten or puppy in the qu
Or dump it in the park as soon as it grows up
and stops being cute.

I will not wait until finals week
to begin doing my homework.

I will not run over any disabled students
while racing my bike through campus.

I will limit my beer consumption to 3 six-packs a day exc
on Saturday, Sunday
and major holidays li
Monday, Tuesday,
Wednesday, Thursda
and Friday.

I will not get arres
for growing pot ir
my closet.
This year, I'll try the
tomato garden.

I will not gamble away my food stamps.
Unless I'm feeling really lucky!

I will look carefully both ways
before running red lights and stop signs on my bicycl

I will not spend my textbook money on party favors. Just parties.

I will stop arguing with my roommates
and house plants over petty political differences.

I will not stand in front of the fireplace
wearing a toga this year.

I will promptly go to the Student Health Center
if I develop any pains or itches in the genital region.
Once there, I will do my level best to infect
the entire staff with whatever personal ailment I have.

**I will write more than
"Out of drugs. Please send money!"**
to my parents this school year.

Love,
Your Studious Son

~January 25, 1979

NEW Courses on TAP for SPRiNG SEMESTER

Look for some **exciting additions** to the **Chico State** curriculum this spring:

Dog Disobedience
Train your mutt to destroy furniture, attack relatives and **bark all night** without stopping. Course is first of its type offered in Chico.

Introduction to Tubing
Learn the fundamentals of littering, **trespassing** and **skinny-dipper watching**. Course includes a special seminar on how to **drown visiting relatives**.

Carnivorous Cooking 101
Best ways to waste food and trick your **vegetarian friends** into eating meat.

Essentials of Beer Brewing
The history of Coors, where to hide a keg in your **dorm room** and how to prevent **yeast infections**.

~ October 26, 1978

How to Win Big in
Strip
Volleyball

One of my favorite sports at Chico was **Strip Volleyball.**

A 50-50 **male-female** ratio works best in my experience. If everyone looks **great naked**, that's even better.

My future wife and I played in an informal league of sorts. We'd gather before a barbecue at the country home of some friends who lived in the sleepover town of **Cohasset**. We invited the **best-looking** grad **students** and **professors** we could find.

Whoever makes a flub has to remove an article of **clothing**. If you're smart, you wear a **baseball cap** and **scarf.** Maybe you had the foresight to bring a **tie, necklace** or **bracelet** to **complement** your **cut-offs.**

These could be a **lifesaver**. **Or maybe** you wore a lifesaver.

In the end, it doesn't matter. **Muffs happen**. Before long, someone is at risk of **losing their shirt**. Or **shorts**. It starts getting tense when you get down to the **bras** and **undies.**

Truth be told, this is when the typical game **petered out**. Someone always had to run off and start the barbecue or something. But it was a good way to get the **sparks flying.**

What **Alums** are Doing
TODAY

Gladys Daniels (class of '47) has been placed in a rundown rest home outside Gridley by her son, Charles Daniels (class of '68). With the "old hen out of his hair," Daniels is excited to be moving into the new singles complex on West Sacramento Avenue. This is the former site of a historically important almond orchard, which was plowed under due to "a regrettable human error" by Charles's thriving construction firm.

Bob Lark (class of '65), until recently head coach of the mighty Cloverdale High School Honey Badgers, was fired for making his team play in their jockstraps after a listless first half in the state basketball finals. He is currently fielding head coaching offers "from three Southeastern Conference powerhouses."

Roberta Johnson (class of '67, Animal Husbandry) has a runaway Rottweiler named Run Tin Tin that's wanted by Animal Control in three counties for terrorizing hikers near Quincy. Johnson believes the vegetarian diet she put her once-docile canine on might have triggered the rampage.

Les Luther (class of '77, Religious Studies) has been anointed a deacon in the fast-growing Santa Cruz Church of Latter-Day Wiccan Weavers. Reverend Luther is known for shouting at the devil in his fiery sermons.

Esteban Trabajar (class of '74, Hispanic Studies and Computer Science) has high hopes for his latest *muy loco* invention: a pocket-sized telephone that can also be used as a typewriter or, get this, a portable computer. Good luck with that, Esteban. Better stick to Hispanic Studies!

~ May 10, 1979 (with some updated references added in July 2020)

CHICO'S
Top Swimming Holes

Locals don't need no stinking maps
to find any of these cool summer **wet spots**:

Butte Hall Hole

Just a **stoner's** throw away from the biggest dorm on
campus. **Where else** but in Chico can you
go skinny-dipping with **real beavers**
between class? Otterly unique!

Bear Hole

That's **Bear** as in Yogi not Bare as in ass-naked.
Nice to visit, but I wouldn't want to **drown** here.

One Mile

Like **Zooport Beach** on the 4th of July, with the hottest
lifeguards in Chico. Look out for **jail bait**.

Diversion Dam

Family friendly. Even the frogs
wear **swimsuits**.

Salmon Hole

The sandy beach is great for **spawning**
after **sundown**. Try not to wake the fish.

Brown's Hole

Swimsuits optional. Tan lines prohibited.
So mellow even the bears are **vegan**.

Devil's Kitchen

Aching back? Try the cold-water
whirlpools. Allergic to **poison oak**?
Scratch this spot.

~ Updated from my original article
in the *Chico News and Review*
on June 14, 1979

Fun-loving rugby major, 20, needs rowdy roommate to share 2-BR dive with killer sound system. Easy stumbling distance to campus and licker stores. I'm fluent in Greek, brew my own brew-skis, and look great in a jockstrap.

Part-time junkie, double-major in armed robbery and purse snatching, seeks supportive household of innocent imbeciles with rich parents. Must not be judgmental.

Born-again Christian, 35, into Genesis and the Book of Job, seeks fellowship in a warm Christian environment. Can pay up to 50 loaves of bread a month. Call Matthew, Mark, Luke or Job CALMS-343-2000.

Ve just put my life together after a messy divorce. You will wash the dishes, take out the trash right now, and choose me as your housing partner before I really get mad. Call Shibboleth at 88-RIGHT-THIS MINUTE.

26-year-old jerk, working on anger issues, seeks meek introvert to share dump on 9th Street. Hurry. Won't last!

Caring home needed for vegan Saint Bernard with huge appetite. Bites small children and hogs the pillow in bed. But loves to haul kegs under his neck!

23

Welcome HOME Wildcats!

Here are some friendly reminders for all the returning students who plan to adopt **new kittens** this school year:

🐾 Cats love fresh chicken, steak and diced goldfish. Steamed **hot dogs**, too. Stock your cellar with a year's supply of canned tuna in case **martial law** is declared.

🐾 You needn't bother with time-wasting chores like housebreaking your pets. They'll find a way to make do.

The following simple precautions will ensure your litter darlings enjoy a safe home:

🐾 Lock all doors and cat doors to keep out intruders.

🐾 Keep your curtains closed at all times. Peek out from behind them periodically.

🐾 **Don't spay**; let your cats **spray**!

🐾 Beware of animal control officers posing as mailmen, social welfare or the power company.

🐾 Keep a **loaded shotgun** by your bedside at all times.

🐾 At the end of the semester, simply release your pets in Bidwell Park. They'll quickly revert to being

Wild Cats!

Next week, I'll share some handy tips about hoarding old magazines and newspapers.

I ♥

Doggy-Style

Do you know what breaks up a **fraternity kegger**
faster than a squad of jealous cops?
Two dogs getting stuck **doggy-style**
will do it every time!

The setting for one such **frisky fiasco** was
the **TKE house** on Chestnut Street. One minute, 300
drunk college students were grooving to a live band
on the lawn, all hoping to **get laid** before midnight.

The next minute, it was just me and a few crestfallen
stragglers staring wistfully at a sea of **empty red cups.**

The guilty **party-poopers** were a **fetching** French
Poodle and desperate Dalmatian, twerking awkwardly
near center stage. They were still locked **groin-to-groin**
in **abject humiliation** when I called it a night.

And to think...
The **conjoined canines** had hooked up only five
minutes earlier. Now they were **screwing the pooch** in
their first **trial separation.** Making matters worse,
both the male and female of the species
had been hoping for a **quickie.**

Talk about a **buzz kill.**

Epidogg

The **mating-dog incident**
happened right after a wet
T-shirt contest I helped judge
at the TKE house.

In a previous chapter,
I moved the action to a more
prestigious lawn.
I hope the Chancellor doesn't
mind the **shout-out!**

25

TALKING TRASH
with a Skinny-Dipper

I caught up with a talkative Public Nudity Major the other day while he was skinny-dipping at **Brown's Hole** in **Upper Bidwell Park**, adopting the native vernacular as best I could.

Q: Whaddup, 'Zilla? How's it hanging?

A: Chillin' where the sun don't shine, brah. Have you met my friend, Monty?
(Points to his crotch with a grand flourish.)
Ta-da!

Q: Impressive. What is it about swimming in the nude that turns you on?

A: I feel so free and natural when I'm nude. Plus, I really enjoy showing off Monty.

Q: What's your secret? Herbs? Surgery? Exercise?

A: Vacuum cleaner!

Q: That sucks. Any other hobbies?

A: I used to be into streaking. Till I lost a step running the **50-yard dash**. What a hassle that turned out to be. Have you ever gotten booked, finger-printed and tried to call a lawyer wearing only Converse? Luckily, my **Dick Pick** and **Moon Shots** were a big hit with the brass.

Q: What are your favorite skinny-dipping spots?

A: It's important to find a secluded location, where you won't make a spectacle of yourself. Next to the **hot dogs** at One Mile on a hot Sunday afternoon is my favorite.

Q: What's the biggest problem skinny-dippers face today? Lack of beaches? Police? Voyeurs?

A: Sunburn. No touching!

Q: Sorry. Do you have any advice for beginners?

A: Look out for snapping turtles, brah!

~ *Butte County Bugle*
July 19, 1977

Naked Truths about
Skinny Dipping

That last interview reminded me of how risky it can be to go full commando in a quasi-public setting.

Why?

Because it sucks to get an erection in public. Same thing goes for **nude beaches**. If you're a **naked guy** hanging out at the old swimming hole with junior, the last thing you want is for him to become a senior.

My advice? Stick to your knitting.

Literally. As in, think about knitting. Or a loved one's funeral. Anything to keep your BB gun in its holster.

The opposite is a problem as well.

Many a naked man standing in cold water has watched his reputation shrink and disappear before his very eyes.

"Hold on there! Where do you think you're going now, little fella?"

Though flying your flag at full mast can be inappropriate, no man in the world wants to see his flag roll up and disappear completely.

What to do?
The opposite of knitting!

In my case, that would mean thinking about a 100% exfoliated Bollywood **lesbian** getting better acquainted with my wife and a day-glow **blond avatar** in one of those interactive psychedelically **colorized porn** movies that are all the rage these days.

"Whoa, Nelly!"

29

Why **Elvin Bishop** Deserves
TENURE (or Ten Years)

Just once, I'd like to see a **Pioneer Week** pass without having to suffer through another Elvin Bishop concert. No offense intended to Mr. Bishop. He's a **fine performer** and probably a **wonderful father**. But how many years in a row do we have to listen to him?

In the past eight years, I think Elvin Bishop has played in about **20 Pioneer Week Concerts**. He spends more time on campus than most students. He has more **pass completions** than the quarterback. Maybe it's time to consider building a home for him on the 20-yard line.

My God. If Elvin plays here again next year, he'll qualify for **tenure**. Next year, instead of listing Bishop's name in the ad, we could save space by saying:

"Who Else?"

The **sad part** is, what this could do to the **student body**. Imagine going home after four years of college and your friends ask, "Wow, did you see any good groups while you were up there?"

"Yeah, man," you reply.

"Elvin Bishop 12 times."

~ Originally published in the *Butte County Bugle*
April 19, 1979

'Fooled Around' &Lost Count

I was making new friends all over town now!

Some 41 years later, trying to keep it real,
I've sent **several emails** to the
Chico Performing Arts Committee
asking how many times Elvin Bishop
actually headlined the annual
Chico State **Spring Concert** on the **Green Series**.

No one has gotten back to me.
So, I'm sticking to my original estimate.

It was at least 1,000.

ALL THE
Big Concerts
You Missed this Summer

The Beatles came together for one night only on June 16 at Nellie's Bar and Grill. Too bad **Yoko** and **Linda** got into a catfight after their first set. Otherwise, **Paul** said, they'd have played all night.

The Rolling Stones rocked **Bidwell Mansion** on July 4th. Unfortunately, the fireworks after the Jumping Jack Flash encore missed the sky completely. What a barnburner that was. To see Mick and the boys Play With Fire in person was the dream of a lifetime for many.

Jimi Hendrix and **Janis Joplin** made a surprise appearance at a fundraiser for the **Drug Abuse Hot Line** on August 1. They were stoned out of their minds, too!

Kiss headlined a three-night stand at **Hooker Oak Elementary School**. The K-5 crowd rock-n-rolled all day and partied every night for the rest of the summer with their $24.99 Kiss-logoed lunch pails.

Finally, sixties psychodelic rocker **Charlie Manson** held several groupies spellbound during a **killer** set at La Salle's. What stage presence!

And you thought Chico was boring in the summer.

~ *Butte County Bugle*
August 31, 1978

32

'Rocky Horror' & the Kid from Gridley

It's Saturday night, 29 degrees out and an 18-year old boy in **high heels, lace panties, pink gloves,** a **black cape** and **blood-red lipstick** is shivering in front of the Senator Theater, waiting to buy his ticket for **The Rocky Horror Picture Show**.

Q: Where' ya from?

A: Gridley.

Q: Gridley? Do you always dress like this?

A: Only on weekends.

Q: What would your dad do if he saw you right now?

A: Probably beat the crap out of me.

The Rocky Horror Picture Show has been attracting block-long lines to the Senator Theater's midnight movies for over two months now. If nothing else, the movie has changed the **underwear-buying habits** of America's adolescents. Half the fans in line Saturday night looked like refugees from a Liberace look-alike contest brought to you by **Frederick's of Hollywood.**

"It's a blast!"
one girl exclaimed.

*"How many other movies can you go to
in your mother's underwear?"*
quipped a manly young tranny dressed as Mae West.

"It's like a giant party,"
said another.

"I just come here to look at the kooks,"
said one fan in his 20s. "It's like going to
San Francisco only you don't have to drive so far."

Fans act out the movie, right along with the characters on screen. They throw rice, shoot squirt guns, throw pieces of toast and shout out lines before the characters on screen can say them. During one scene, everyone swarms to the front of the theater to do a wild dance called **The Time Warp.**

Here's how to make the most of these precious moments:

WHAT TO WEAR

- Black stockings, silk panties, garter belt, pink heels
- Sequined leather vest *(falsies optional)*
- Black wig and Dracula cape
- Pearl necklace
- Blood red lipstick, smeared thick *(fangs optional)*
- White face paint *(beauty marks optional)*

WHAT TO BRING

- **Rice**, preferably Uncle Ben's.
- **Toast**, four slices burned to a crisp to promote smooth flying.
- **A dirty mouth.** Be sure to brush up on your cuss words before the show so you can shout plenty of profanities at the screen.
- **Bodyguard.** This will keep you from getting beat up as you walk to your car after the movie.

~ Originally published in the
Chico News and Review on November 16, 1978

Squirt Gun ✓

Toast ✓

Rice ✓

A Taste of Honey

In spite of the nay-sayers, I persevered and sent my very worst efforts to the San Francisco Chronicle and Los Angeles Times. Imagine my surprise when they printed and paid me for them!

Speaking of honey, do you know how U.S. interrogators got **Saddam Hussein** to talk? It wasn't by **torture**. They **bribed** him with gourmet **honey**.

Da' kine!

They got it from **Lebanon** or somewhere. It was so **delicious** it gave him a **buzz**. Look it up. Anyway, I just wanted to make sure you learned something from this book. I also needed to pay off the **Beatles riff** in the headline.

Back to the SF Chronicle and LA Times ... If only their famous columnists **Herb Caen** and **Jack Smith** could see me now, they'd still be alive today.

My first big-league hit, print-wise, starts and ends on the next page.

Revenge of the Sequels

New blockbusters coming soon
to a theater near you:

The Grape Nuts of Wrath

Delinquent descendants of the **Joad** family move to
Battle Creek, Michigan, and become **cereal killers**.
Stars **Ernest** and **Julio Gallo** as leaders of
the infamous Kellogg's Gang.

Ripped Man Wrinkle

Sylvester Stallone punches his way to glory as a
100-year-old prizefighter.

Robinson Clouseau

The bumbling French inspector is outwitted
by **Gilligan** and the gang after the weather
starts getting rough and the **Minnow**
is lost on a three-hour tour.

Moby Dick 2

Shamu busts out of **Sea World**
and terrorizes **water parks**
throughout the Southland.
Breakthrough **acting**
performance by Shamu
under the direction
of Lloyd Bridges. Made
a **big splash** at Cannes.

~ Originally published in
the *Los Angeles Times*
on December 2, 1979

The Warning Labels

We Need

ALCOHOL
May lead to head-on collisions, suspension of driving privileges and abrupt termination of employment. Tastes pretty good when mixed with **FERMENTED** hops or grapes, though.

CANNABIS
Makes you creative, stupid and hungry for donuts at the same time. **HIGHLY RECOMMENDED** for aspiring comics to bake in brownies and offer to audience members 1 hour before giving your first live performance.

CANNABIS GROWING
This is going to be a lot of work, and you might have to spend **2-5 YEARS** letting someone else tend the garden while you catch up on your reading. Have you considered growing parsley?

COCAINE
May result in felony arrest or a **FLACCID PENIS**. Sometimes both.

PARSLEY, SAGE, ROSEMARY & THYME
Use sparingly. Caused Simon to sue Garfunkel and makes **HORNY** graduates want to sleep with Mrs. Robinson.

OPIOIDS
Cause constipation and **SUDDEN FUNERALS**. Make you feel yucky for days when you run out.

WARNING LABELS
You're not going to read this anyway. So go ahead and do your thing. Just don't come **CRYING** back to me later.

AMBIEN
Leads to **SLEEPWALKING** and a sudden urge for popcorn at 3 in the morning.

Added at 3:05 a.m. on July 13, 2020.
"What's burning?"

~ Originally published in the **Butte County Bugle** on August 23, 1979

A Farewell to A{l}monds

Some activities are unique to Chico.
Meaning, I've never heard of anyone
anywhere else doing them.

For example:

- **Taking a sweat.** This means hanging out and sweating naked among friends in a makeshift outdoor sauna.

- **Tubing.** Chico's the national champion!

- **Raking leaves** into a pile and burning them for no discernible reason.

- **Pronouncing Chico's** second-biggest cash crop as **amonds**, not **almonds**. Locals say shaking the tree **"knocks the L out of them."** Get it? So, if you're ever interrogating a suspect and want to find out if she's **really from Chico**, just ask her to explain how she picks and pronounces her **favorite nuts**.

As you can see, I was running out of bad material.

Time for some sexy gardening tips!

Mamas, Don't Let Your ZUCCHINIS→ Grow Up to Be WEENIES→

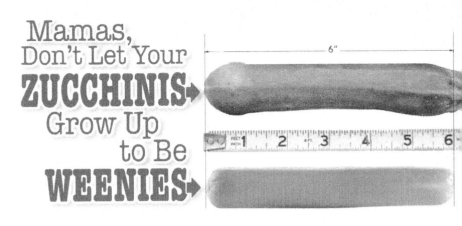

A good rule of thumb for the **summer gardener** is never let your zucchini grow any larger than a **lubricated plastic device** in the approximate size and shape of an **Oscar Mayer Weiner**.

That's because a zucchini is one of those versatile vegetables that **plunges** in value as it grows larger. As soon as it gets bigger than a **baby's head**, it turns into a **fruitcake**.

Here's something they should tell you on **freshman orientation** day:

When you give an overgrown zucchini to a neighbor in Chico, **ring the doorbell and run!**

One **huge** zucchini I know got passed around the neighborhood for two years before getting **squashed**.

Back to your fascination with **organic sex toys**. I'm told the right-size zucchini does the trick in a jam.

Carrots are a good alternative for those getting bi on a **small celery**.

Slipping
Out of Town
on a
Banana Slug

**You'll probably agree
it was time to
move on.**

Destination: Santa Cruz!

PART 2

Good Times
in
Santa
Cruz

JUNE 25, 1980

THE ENTERTAINMENT MAGAZINE OF

Willie Nels

S

Strung

Sr

GOOD

TIMES

45

Wising Up

After Chico, I moved to Santa Cruz and became managing editor of **Good Times**, a thriving entertainment weekly. Once again, my writing was an instant hit with the community.

"Dear C L Smith –
Re: the **Shogun** parody. Your pseudo-interviews are disgusting. You owe your entire community an apology."

"Dear Editor –
Your bogus counter-cultural posturing shows through glaringly in the so-called humor articles by C L Smith.
Wise up!"

Dang.

20, 1980

LETTERS

Not Funny

I'm writing to register a complaint about your March 12th so-called "humor" issue. That much of it was written on an embarrassingly juvenile level is not even the point (has C L Smith no sense of subtlety? What's even more bothersome is the
... Smith

as so
gynecol
hairy
talki
men
ster
guy

H

Riding 'Shogun'
with LORD TORANAGA

We caught up with Lord Toranaga last week during a break from his sword-swallowing practice in Little Tokyo. Translations provided by the lovely Lady Mariko:

Q: Is it true the Japanese stole the whole Samurai concept from John Belushi?
(Lord Toranaga unsheathes his sword and positions it next to reporter's head.)

LT: Hi-yaaaa!

LM: Lord Toranaga suggests you rephrase the question. And hurry!

Q: Okay. What's with all the raw fish?

LM: Lord Toranaga say with only one hibachi in all of 17th century Japan, you'd love sushi, too.

Q: Would LT advise young people to take up being a Shogun as a career path?

LM: Yes! As long they don't mind the sudden-death retirement plan.

Q: There he goes talking about death again. Why is the Lord so ready to die all the time?

LM: Toranaga-sama says you are a garlic-eating linthead. In 17th century Japan, there was no TV, no air conditioning, no take-out. You'd be ready to die, too.

Q: Okay then, why did he and the boys take so many baths together?

LM: Toranaga-sama say whole country full of dust, hard to keep clean without a vacuum cleaner. Bath also great place to look at naked geisha girls.

Q: But if bathing was so sacred, why did he have two of Dr. Kildare's men boiled alive over a hot tub?

LM: Lord Toranaga-sama say nobody perfect.

Q: Just one more question: What is Lord Toranaga's favorite shampoo?

LM: Lord Toranaga say, Head & Shoulders. Starting with yours!

~ Originally published
in the *Santa Cruz Good Times*
on September 18, 1980
Co-written with my GT colleague
Richard Stone.

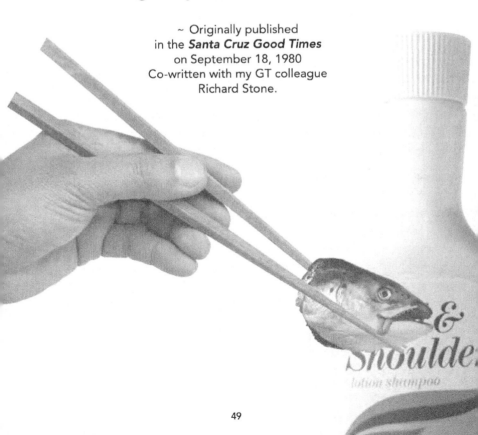

A Swinger's Paradise

Oh, to be young and stupid again.

While I was editor of **Good Times**, I got to do a lot of interesting **new-age** stuff. Like attending a couples-only workshop on giving **naked massages** to strangers. I brought my wife at the time along for the ride.

The weekend retreat was at a secluded **nudist colony** in the Santa Cruz Mountains called **Getting in Touch**. We were in our late 20s and must've looked pretty-pretty-pretty good to a couple of **horny swingers** from LA. The **attractive wife** was soon teaching me the finer points of Trager massage while her **suave hubby** was demonstrating his **magic hands** to my **naked wife**.

Fair's fair, right?

The four of us were soon inseparable. Comparing our progress. Sharing **repartee** during the breaks. As the day went on, we got more **in touch** with each new technique and **muscle group** we explored.

It was during the **Naked Lunch** that the couple started talking about how much fun they'd had at **Plato's Retreat**. We soon learned this was a famous swinger's club in New York. Then came the **innuendos** about the fantastic time they had with all the **beautiful people** they met there. We'd probably enjoy the Plato's Retreat experience, too, if we cared to join them on their next visit.

New friends! ♥

"**G**ee, what a friendly couple," we remarked after declining their polite invitation to join them in their cabin for a nightcap after dinner. Though 20 years younger, we were **getting tired**. Day two of the seminar started at 10 a.m. sharp the next day, so we had to be up at the **crack of Dawn**. This was also the other wife's name, so that was a poor choice of words on my part.

The next day, our new friends **Don** and **Dawn** gave us the **cold shoulder**, literally, as they set their sights on another young couple. **Horror of horrors**, my wife and I had to spend Sunday massaging each other. Been there, done that.

Then it dawned on us.

The reason we'd suddenly turned into **yesterday's meat** with our new friends.

Duh!

PHOTO: JACK FISHER

They weren't just talking about the **joys of swinging**. They wanted us to get on the **swings** in their **cabin** with them!

How stupid could we be?

I dutifully wrote an article for **Good Times** about the **amazing massage methods** we'd learned in the flesh at Getting in Touch. It was legit, too. **Certified Trager** techniques and all.

But then, as I got wiser and better connected around Santa Cruz, I learned what **every swinger** within 500 miles already knew.

The Naked Massage Seminar was a Swinger's Paradise!

Like I said, oh, to be young and stupid again. Why, if we could go back in time and do that weekend all over again, my **27-year-old wife** and I probably would have chickened out just like we did the first time.

Time for more bedroom hijinks!

~ Based on my original experience and article
in the *Santa Cruz Good Times*
on September 18, 1981

2 Long Weeks of Celibacy

What's it like, when you're happily married and have a **healthy sex life**, to take a two-week vow of **celibacy**? After a recent quarrel, my wife Nancy decided it was time for me to find out ... **first-hand**.

Following is a day-by-dismal-day account of the experience:

1-3 The first three days, from **Monday** to **Wednesday**, were no problem, since during that part of the week my **love monkey** and I are usually too busy to think about sex anyway. So it was business as usual with no **hanky-panky** even if I'd wanted to.

4 **Thursday** night, with the weekend in sight, the first sign of trouble **popped up**. Literally. We went out for **ice cream**.

5 The big test came on day five, a **Friday**. After enjoying a **candlelit dinner** and bottle of wine ... big mistake ... I think even my **pouting partner** was tempted to end my **probation**.

But her will power prevailed, and we settled for **Fantasy Island** and two **Sominex**. It was opposite sides of the bed and keep my hands to myself, or else.

Or else what?

Never mind.
I didn't have the balls to find out.

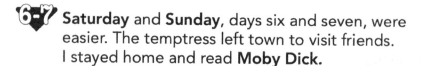

6-7 **Saturday** and **Sunday**, days six and seven, were easier. The temptress left town to visit friends. I stayed home and read **Moby Dick**.

8-10 Days eight through ten, **Monday** through **Wednesday**, passed quickly enough. I worked late and tried to catch up on the articles in my old copies of **Playboy**.

That was another mistake.

11 Then things got tough. **Thursday** night, after a long day of frustration, I had a rapturous **X-rated** dream.

12

13 **Friday** night it was a **nightmare**.

By **Saturday** I could think of nothing else, so I called a **priest** and asked him how he did it. He said to try **prayer**, which at least kept **my hands busy**.

14

On **Sunday**, the last day of the ordeal, I figured I'd channel all my **pent-up sexual energy** into writing the Great American Novel.

Unfortunately, this **stupid story** was all I could come up with.

Mercifully, my partner winked and allowed me to advance the plot. We **popped** open a bottle of champagne and got busy conceiving a **Happy Ending**.

~ Originally published in
Santa Cruz Good Times
September 11, 1980

A Beginner's Glossary of
Common Sexual Terms

Developing a **rich vocabulary** will pay many dividends in the years ahead. Here are **69** of the most **common sexual terms** worth **memorizing** as you grow into the **full flower** of adulthood.
Give or take a **Dirty Dozen**.

aural sex *(n)* An obscene phone call.

basstard *(n)* Illegitimate game fish.

boyeur *(n)* Adolescent Peeping Tom.

cellabacy *(n)* Prolonged period of sexual abstinence due to jail term.

circumdecision *(n)* Parental dilemma of whether or not to circumcise a newborn boy.

circumderision *(n)* Locker-room tradition of teasing uncircumcised boys. Or vice versa.

clumsilingus *(n)* Cunnilingus performed in a clumsy, awkward or idiotic fashion.

contrareceptive *(adj)* Female state of sexual readiness characterized by the prior insertion of a diaphragm or other contraceptive device. Also: Female state of sexual unreadiness due to watching her favorite TV show.

condomundrum *(n)* The question faced by couples of whether to slow down and put on a condom or not.

dickoration *(n)* A tiny jockstrap used by male strippers.

Dill Dohhh! *(n)* Phallic-shaped dill pickle used as a sex toy.*

fallatio *(n)* Bravado act of fellatio performed while skydiving.

fasterBayShun *(n)* Masturbating in a hurry with your eyes shut under a boardwhack by an estuary.

fantaSIZE *(v)* Tendency of males to imagine they have a larger-than-average penis.

goynecology *(n)* The branch of medicine dealing with the sexual problems and diseases of horny gentiles.

gropie *(n)* A pervert who gropes strangers in crowds.

hejockulation *(n)* Ejaculation, usually premature, by a well-endowed athlete.

hijackulation *(n)* Ejaculation in a jet being hijacked.

honeymooning *(v)* Baring one's rear end on a wedding night.

insex *(n)* Two or more insects, such as wasps, caught in the act of sexual coupling by a shocked human observer.

intercoarse (n) Intercourse performed with inadequate lubrication.

lickluster *(adj)* Showing a lack of talent or enthusiasm during oral sex. As in, "The woman complained about her boyfriend's lickluster performance."

lingeraid *(n)* Intimate wear designed to arouse desire in a bored or boring partner.

lustration *(n)* An extended period of sexual arousal not followed by a satisfactory orgasm.

manager a trois *(n)* A sexual triangle involving three managers working for the same organization.

mermade *(n)* In ancient Greek legend, a nyphomaniac mermaid.

moregasm *(n)* One of multiple orgasms.

ourgasm *(n)* Simultaneous orgasm.

poorgasm *(n)* A lousy orgasm.

preg-nyuck-nyucky *(n)* Comical act of making love when more than seven months pregnant.

prostidude *(n)* Male hooker.

pros-tit-tuition *(n)* Fee paid to a college-bound prostitute.

reserection *(n)* In males, the pride-swelling accomplishment of getting it up more than once during a single lovemaking session.

ridickulous *(re dick' you less)* *(adj)* Disparaging description of any erect penis under three inches in length.

rubber check *(n)* The act of a couple stopping in the middle of intercourse to make sure the rubber is still on.

screw diver *(n)* A horny scuba diver.

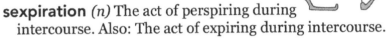

sexaggeration *(v)* Typical male act of embellishing the truth when describing a sexual adventure to another male. Also: Typical female act of moaning louder than necessary to impress her partner while having a fake orgasm.

sexpiration *(n)* The act of perspiring during intercourse. Also: The act of expiring during intercourse.

sinpathy *(n)* Shared sense of guilt felt by a couple when cheating on their partners. See also: "squilt."

squilt *(n)* The state of not feeling as guilty as you think you should after doing something wrong or kinky you know you'll do again as soon as you possibly can.

stagravation *(n)* State of aggravated horniness caused by watching porn.

suckond *(n)* Elapased time it takes a premature ejaculator to reach orgasm when receiving oral sex.

suckretary *(n)* A secretary who performs oral sex on his or her boss. Also: A secretary whose work performance sucks.

sucktion *(n)* The pleasurable pressure on one's genitals created during oral sex.

tasticle *(n)* A testicle with sweetener on it.

titilibation *(n)* Ridiculous male act of making "goo-goo-gaga" sounds and pretending to nurse like a baby while weaning off an ample female breast.

vice clod *(n)* A nerdy vice squad officer.

"whipping up a batch" *(v)* See 'fasterbation.'

whoreified *(v)* Male act of faking moral outrage when propositioned by a prostitute in front of his wife or girlfriend.

x-tra *(n)* Actor or actress playing a bit part in a pornographic movie. A good summer job if you can get it.

Catching Up on the CRIME REPORTS

Here are the crime reports you missed
if you blinked last month:

Traffic Stop Nabs Dead Head

A UC Santa Cruz student was pulled over and arrested
Saturday for having too many **Grateful Dead** stickers on his
Volvo. **Public nuisance** charges were added after police
searched the car without a warrant and found a **large cache**
of tie-dyed T-shirts, Jerry Garcia posters and raw patchouli.

Street Musician Sings Off Key

A tone-deaf street musician was arrested downtown
Wednesday on charges of playing a guitar badly, singing out
of tune and impersonating James Taylor. Police arrested
Liddle Rascal, 44, after his throaty rendition of **Fire and Rain**
sickened several passersby.

Suspect Gives Cops the Slip

A case of Vaseline, two dozen rubber gloves, five boxes
of **Preparation H** and a year's supply of Fleet enemas were
reported stolen from **Karma Pharmarama** on Sunday night.
The thief scrawled the words, "I'm a desperate man!" on
the restroom wall before making a clean getaway.

~ *Santa Cruz Good Times*
March 27, 1980

Recipes for Disaster

Couch Potato Supreme

4 well-seasoned sports fans (plump, not firm)
8 bags of Doritos (jumbo size or 12-pack)
4 quarts guacamole (California heirloom)
1 remote control (extra batteries optional)
8 poached golf tees (Ping or Taylor Made)
1 pinch baseball resin (pre DH)
6 strips bacon (NFL pigskin, no seams showing)
2 finely ground hockey pucks (kosher)
1 pair Air Jordans (never worn, keep in box)
Bake at 420° next to a big-screen TV for 8 hours.
Repeat 52 weeks of the year.

Dieter's Delight

1 cup tap water
1 celery string
1 chicken bone (cleaned)
Boil tap water till it evaporates, leaving just the
bone and celery string.
Add additional chicken bones if desired.
Serve piping hot.

Junk Food Jam

1 bag of stale potato chips
1 quart of soda pop
4 melted chocolate bars, any brand

Throw solid items with cellophane wrappers into large salad bowl.

Douse contents with soda pop.

Bake at 450° until contents explode.

Serve to surviving guests.

The Hangover

1 hair of dog
(sip and let marinate in stomach 30 minutes)

Another hair of dog
(drink in 3 gulps and let marinate for 10 minutes)

What the hell, another hair of dog
(chug in single gulp)

Continue as desired throughout day and night.

Repeat next morning before noon.

Miss work on Monday.
Schedule AA meeting for Wednesday.

~ Santa Cruz Good Times
November 15, 1979

Look, ma.
Now I'm writing with no hands!

Getting Lit on
LiTERaTURE

Did you know?

Emily Bronte wrote **Wuthering Heights**
while dangling by her ankles
from the top of Winchester Cathedral.

Jack London was a pyromaniac
long before writing **To Build a Fire**.

John Steinbeck wrote
The Grapes of Wrath in a single day,
while nursing a severe hangover.

J.D. Salinger's original career aspirations included
playing baseball and baking bread. He failed at
both and setttled on being a **Catcher in the Rye**.

Ernest Hemingway wrote **A Farewell to Arms**
after suffering an unfortunate accident
in his high-school shop class.

John Milton was blind as a bat out of hell
when he wrote **Paradise Lost**.

The Bible was rejected by 20 major publishers
before God gave up and had it printed Himself.

~ Santa Cruz Good Times
September 11, 1980

ACCIDENTS
WILL HAPPEN

Be prepared for your next mishap:

- **Is your hair clean, combed and shampoo-fresh?**
  Nothing grosses out a brain surgeon like
  a bit of dandruff.

- **How about your underwear?**
  This is the first thing most doctors and nurses check.
  Don't be a laughingstock!

- **Have you brushed, flossed and gargled today?**
  You'll want your breath to be fresh if an attractive
  stranger gives you mouth-to-mouth resuscitation.

- **Have you destroyed all your kinky magazines?**
  Nothing puts a damper on a funeral like knowing
  the deceased was a raving pervert.

- **How recent was your last manicure?**
  Don't make the morgue worry
  about something so pedi.

~ *Santa Cruz Good Times*
June 26, 1980

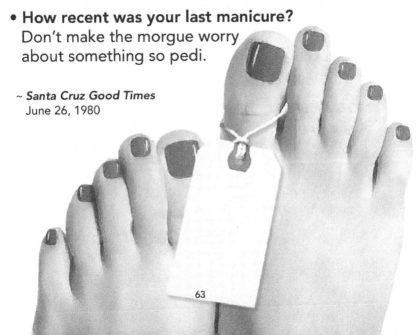

63

Movie-Watching
Made Easy

Going to the movie theater alone.
Everyone wonders if you're a lonely sociopath. Usually, the answer is yes. Why else would you be sitting alone in the dark watching Love Story?

Going to the movie theater with a buddy.
Knock elbows and worry that everyone will think you're gay? Or leave a seat empty and look like insecure wimps? **Answer:** Sit close and hold hands!

Sitting next to a compulsive talker.
This can be dangerous except in certain ethnic neighborhoods, where everybody talks back to the screen anyway. **Solution?** Hide in the restroom.

Tall
Scrunch down and twist into a pretzel if necessary.

Short
Bring a pillow.

Heavy-set
Stay away from the snack bar.

~ *Santa Cruz Good Times*
  January 3, 1980

PART 3

BALLS
Beyond
Walls

Let the **GOOD TIMES** Roll

After more Good Times in **Santa Cruz** and a stint as Communications Manager for the **Cambridge Diet** people in foggy **Monterey**, I moved to **Orange County**, where my marketing career really took off.

I met some super-smart businesspeople among the colorful **scam artists** there. Soon I was crossing paths with the very elite of **Hollywood's B, C** and **D** lists with an occasional **A-lister** for good measure.

Which one are YOU?

CELEBRITY JEOPARDY!

Here are some **celebs I've met in person** who were really cool and charismatic even when they didn't have to be. By going public with this, I'm just doing my part to keep celebrities on their toes. They never know when they're going to end up in a book on somebody's **cool/not cool list**.

So better watch out, better not pout!

Super Cool

Pamela Anderson (Golden Globes in Hollywood)

David Arquette (major props)

Chester Bennington (backstage at KROQ Acoustic Christmas, sweet guy, so sad)

Barbi Benton (Hef's true love and I could see why)

Rachel Bilson (at peak of **The OC,** total sweetheart; played the mean girl on show, in person was the opposite)

Kobe Bryant (much nicer off the court than on)

Dyan Cannon (sweetheart)

Jamie Foxx (at **Sports Illustrated** annual swimsuit party in Miami, **lit it up!**)

Jesse Jane (porn star, so cool, **Spider Club** in Hollywood)

Paris Hilton
(on multiple occasions including her **30th birthday party** in Hollywood. **Total sweetheart!**)

Magic Johnson
(but you knew that)

Kira Reed
(adult actress, socialite, author, love her!)

Stryker on KROQ (Rock of the 20s!)

Dennis Rodman (unofficial Mayor of Newport Beach, **US ambassador to North Korea**, cool guy)

Gretchen Rossi (to die for)

Brad Pitt (said hello and tipped a beer my way at a urinal during a **KROQ Acoustic Xmas**)

Iggy Pop (sat in my lap at the **Whiskey A-Go-Go**)

John Stamos (at **Playboy** mansion and backstage with friends in his dressing room after **Bye Bye Birdie** in NYC)

No Complaints

George W Bush (had the good ol' boy patter down pat, at a **Republican fundraiser** in LA)

Bill Clinton (crushin' it with the ladies, at a **Democratic fundraiser** in LA)

Gerald Ford (at a fundraiser for something in **Beverly Hills**)

"Hef" (met twice at the mansion;
in his pajamas or bathrobe, I forget which;
many other guests wore neither)

Steve Jones (of the **Sex Pistols** at
Key Club in West Hollywood didn't throttle me
after I mistook him for a member of the Stranglers)

Tommy Lee (hitting on Pink at
a **Motorola launch party**)

Anna Nicole Smith
(**Golden Globes**, totally wasted, her not me)

Prince (chill and nodding off at a private party in
the **West Hollywood Standard** after the **Grammys**)

Gene Simmons (chill, not a jerk,
at **Sonoma Raceway**)

Ivanka Trump (friendly, hot, at a
Celebrity Apprentice party in NYC, ignored Jared)

Total Jerks

Mischa Barton (at height of **The OC**,
piece of work; she played the sweet girl on show;
was **opposite in person**)

Reggie Jackson (**Angel Stadium**. In fairness the girl
I was with asked for his autograph
while he was loosening up in the on-deck circle
with the bases loaded)

Sean Penn (tried to pick a fight with me
at **Sunset Tower bar** because I'm taller than he is.
But how cool and on brand of him it was to do that, right!)

FOR GUYS ONLY

Women, Please Don't Read this Chapter

If you're a female, or even a female impersonator, please stop reading this section right now and move along to the next chapter.

Trust me. You wouldn't be interested in any of this next stuff anyway.

Cool?
Thanks for understanding.

Hey, Guys.
How about those amazing birthday BJs we get like clockwork every year!

Why, in our household, we've expanded this patriotic tradition to include Christmas, Easter, Hanukkah, Halloween, **Hump Day**, **Over-the-Hump Day**, Valentine's Day, MLK Day, **MILF Day,** Groundhog Day, 4/20, my wife's birthday, Our Anniversary, 9/11, Cyber Monday, Super Tuesday, **Weblow Wednesday**, Thirsty Thursday, Black Friday, **Bad Santa Saturday** and any other day of the year if that be my fair lady's wish.

But remember.
Loose lips sink ships.
Got it?

Guy code.
This is just between us.

Not the
Birthday Surprise
I was Expecting

The **sunrise surprise** didn't work out as planned this year. My wife and every other woman in the world ignored my **specific instructions** not to read that last chapter.

As for the book's so-called **soft cover**, the entire lower-left corner of the binding **isn't soft at all**.

I should be fine after another two weeks of **celibacy** or once the **bruises** heal, whichever comes **last**.

All of those upcoming **holidays** have been **canceled** till further notice, too.

Dang.

'Balls Behind Walls

This expression will serve you well in the coming years. It's great for describing a **blowhard** yelling at what he'd do if he could only get his hands on those **protesters** or **rednecks** or **gangbangers** or **mosquitos** or his **boss** or whatever's aggravating him at the moment.

Why, he'd, he'd show them a thing or two.

Namely, that he has actually left his **balls behind walls.**

A good friend and executive mentor of mine at **AirTouch Mike Benvenuti**, laughed so hard on first hearing this expression that 25 years later he can still give a blow-by-blow recap of the meeting we were in.

A boss of mine and peer of Mike's turned **meek as a mouse** in a big showdown with headquarters after bragging that he was going to **take those A-holes to the woodshed.**

Now just let me get my hands on the next **nasty email** that turns up in my mailbox. Why, I'll show that **email** a thing or two. In the meantime, how about those **cute lesbians** frolicking with my wife **on the beach** in Bali!

Put on a
Little Make-up

A Hollywood celebrity whose name I won't mention
stayed overnight at our house a couple of times.
When we all met in the morning for **breakfast**,
my wife and I couldn't believe our eyes!

A **complete stranger** we'd
never seen before was
relaxing in a **bathrobe**
and **curlers** in our
kitchen. This **lovely
creature** with the
darling freckles and
vaguely **familiar
dimples** spoke and
laughed just like our
visiting **celebrity friend**.
But she looked nothing
at all like the **beautiful
starlet** we knew from TV and
had shared a **nightcap** with just
a few hours earlier.

The **mystery guest's** identity was
revealed when our celebrity friend emerged
from her shower and morning constitutional.
She was dressed to the nines and looked just
like the **famous person** we knew from our TV
and smartphones again. Her **miraculous
metamorphosis** at our house that morning just
goes to show what a little makeup in the morning
will do to transform a woman from **girl-next-door
lovely** to **drop-dead gorgeous**.

Embarrassing Moments

Luckily, they didn't kill or ruin me.
I may have even learned something. Let's see!

'Him and I'

Situation: While being interviewed for a job teaching English at a **prominent university**, I answered a question by saying, "Him and I got along great."

Result: Epic fail! Fortunately, I got the job anyway, thanks to my **faculty advisors** pleading that I suffered from temporary idiocy due to being nervous.

Lesson: Pay attention in grammar school.
(Thank you, Dr. Downes, Tom Reck and Clark Brown!)

'Is that all I am being charged with?'

Situation: After I drove off the road and totaled the family station wagon while freaking out on **jimson weed**, which someone had spiked my punch with at a high school **graduation party**, and appearing for morning arraignment in a crowded courtroom, the judge said I was being charged with **reckless driving**. Then he asked if I had anything to say for myself.

"Is that ALL I'm being charged with?"
I inquired, idiotically.

"What else did you DO?"
rejoined the judge.

My parents shook their heads, miserably, as the courtroom erupted in laughter.

Result: A misdemeanor conviction for reckless driving and making a **stupid opening statement** in court.

Lesson: Stay the hell away from **jimson weed**!

'I'm sorry. I completely forgot what I was going to say right now.'

Situation: Going **braindead** before delivering the punch line I'd planned for the clever point I was making in front of 200 fellow wireless executives.

Result: Hiding out in my **hotel room** till my boss called and said, "Shake it off, you've done worse."

Lesson: Remember the **punch line**!

Tin Foiled

**It really hurts
to bite into a clump of
tinfoil.**

Heavy-Duty Reynolds Wrap
is the worst!

NOT Getting Rich Quick

All those debacles remind me of the many **Get Rich Quick** schemes I tried that didn't get me rich, period.

The best of the worst included:

- Personalized love letters from your very own imaginary lover!

- Selling autographed portraits of Jesus via mail order.

- A DIY Hemorrhoid Cure. This last one deserves its very own chapter!

A Handy Cure
for
'Rhoid Rage'

Following poor sales of the signed **Jesus portraits**, my next **Get Rich Quick** plan was to write a book on how to cure hemorrhoids in the privacy of your own home.

It worked like magic!

The cure did, that is. Maybe the book would've sold like **hotcakes**. But I was soon too embarrassed to find out. The cure itself was the **ingenious revelation** that you could push those pesky party-crashers right back where they came from with the help of a **soothing Tuck** or two.

No muss, no fuss.

Meanwhile, two of my brothers and a sister-in-law had thanked me profusely for this handy piece of **medical advice**. Perhaps, dear reader, you too will appreciate this **grand epiphany** I'm sharing with you one day.

80

There was just one problem with my latest **Get Rich Quick** plan. Have you ever gone to a publisher and asked them to print a 14-page book explaining how to cure **your own hemorrhoids**?

I could hardly contain my excitement when the **attractive female** print rep and her **beaming foreman** presented a mock-up of my **masterpiece**.
They'd taken the liberty of adding a cocked pistol underneath the florid title.

Once we all **stopped laughing,** I decided to stick a fork in the project.

Ouch!

You might say I just put my scheme on the **backburner** for 30 years. Until the publication of the **best-seller** you're holding in your **Golden Fingers** right now.

And look at all the other good stuff that's included for the list price this time.

P.S. Golden Fingers was a working title I rejected.

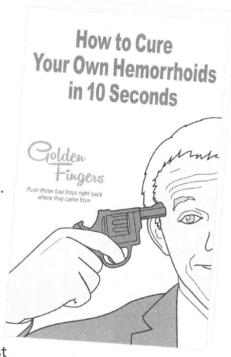

Always have
an EXIT Plan

Guess what corporate America
isn't a huge fan of?

Fistfights in the company cafeteria, for one thing.
Live lavalier mics in the restroom can be a problem, too.
Naked Toddler Olympics in the employee
day-care center. Fuggedaboutit.

Executives with **big salaries** once they reach a **certain age**.
You can bet your **401K**.

Fortunately, a former chief executive honcho and now
good friend, **Brian Jones**, had schooled me years earlier.

Always have an exit plan.

Mine was to get back to my Chico roots as
a highly acclaimed regional author.

Check me out now, brah!

Why I Hate Opioids

Take a morbid quiz with me. My answers are included:
How many people can you name
who've overdosed and died on one of the following:

Cannabis?

Only **Willie Nelson** and **Snoop Dogg**.
And they're not even dead yet.

Mushrooms?

Not even **Gollum**. Though he must've eaten a
gob of bad ones.

Peyote?

Maybe **Carlos Castaneda**, but only in a very trippy dream.

LSD?

Perhaps **Timothy Leary**. But it just as likely
gave him five extra years.

Viagra

John Holmes?

Food

Mama Cass?

Opioids?

John Belushi	Heath Ledger	River Phoenix
Lenny Bruce	Cory Monteith	Elvis Presley
Chris Farley	Jim Morrison	Prince
Janis Joplin	Tom Petty	Hank Williams

That's not counting the ones I know personally,
including an **older brother**.

Here are some blank spaces for you to write the names of **opioid victims** you **miss and loved**:

1. _____

2. _____

3. _____

Easy-peasy, right?

You'll find this is a good way to assess almost any similar issue or situation. Recall from your own experience how many people you've **known personally** and can actually name who've experienced any of the following events.

Again, I'll give you my answers:

- Struck by lightning: **0**
- Kidnapped by aliens: **0**
- Won the Lottery: **0**
- Kidnapped: **0**
- Done something stupid: **95** and counting
- Were annoyed by a lousy driver: **742** times
- Times you've annoyed other drivers: **742** times
- Witnessed road rage: **289** times
- Came close to committing road rage: **289** times
- Committed road rage: **1/2** a time
- Known someone who was arrested: **7**
- Known someone who was arrested twice in one day: **1**
- Known someone who was struck by a car while riding a bicycle: **7**
- Known someone who's had twins: **3**
- Given birth to a litter: **7** (4 cats, 2 dogs, 1 gerbil)
- Known and can name someone who has overdosed on opioids: See long list above.

Opioids also leave you **constipated**. This is why the best anti-drug tagline for this killer might be:

Just Say No to Feeling Like You're Full of Crap

POPULAR PASTIMES
that SUCK

Hot Air Balloons
The roaring flame thrower above your head
is the first sign something's off. The **power line**,
freeway or **cow-pie** you're heading for is the next clue
you've picked a bad outing.

Zip Lines
More dangerous than you think!
Look at the **welts, scars
and missing limbs** of the
helpful attendants before you zip.

Studio Audience Member
It's a lot of work to applaud on cue.
Over and over till the producers think you've got it right
Louder, people!

Scuba Diving in Cold Water
Two guys I know had heart attacks just
trying to fit into their **wetsuits**.
And this was before their meet-and-greet
with a **great white**.

Threesomes
Someone's always getting left out.

Orgies
These **suck** in more ways than one. Trust me.

Your **MUSIC** Knows

WHAT YOU DID LAST SUMMER

Have you ever stopped to wonder if you're gay?
This handy home-test kit will tell you in a jiffy.
Say the first thing that pops into your head:

1. How many songs by Cher can you name?

If you can name only **1**, you are a:
Certified Millennial

If you can name up to **2** Cher songs, you are a:
Certified Gen-Xer

If you can name up to **3** Cher songs, you are a:
Certified Boomer

If you enjoy dressing up as a Gypsy,
Tramp and Indian chief, you are:
Gay as a Goose!

This algorithm is amazing, right?

Having gay pets is cool, too!

Being a 50-year-old **Cher fan**?
Now you're really
licking the envelope.

But who am I to judge?

2. How many Judy Garland movies can you name?

If you draw a blank after
The Wizard of Oz:
Simon says, you're definitely
NOT gay.

3. Here's a fool-proof way to see if you're a lesbian:

You went to Lilith Fair:
Calculating data
You went to Lilith and love K.D. Lang:
Bi-curious
You went to Lilith, love K.D. Lang and slept with
Tegan and Sara:
Bingo!

4. How many times have you seen any of the following performers?

Anthrax
Megadeth
Metallica
Slayer
System of a Down
Kimberly Guilfoyle

If the answer is more than once,
hearing aids start for $2,000 at Costco.
I said, **HEARING AIDS start for $2,000 at COSTCO.**

Told-ya this worked!

Next week I'll introduce my home-testing kit
for bi-curious **Rednecks**
and **Born-Again Christians.**

The Lighter Side of the Covid-19 Pandemic

Villains that Didn't Make the CUT

These are some notorious evil-doers that history forgot:

Dragula

The Mommy

Attila the Hung

The Hillside Flosser

Jack the Stripper

Lizzie Boredom

Jay-Z James

Ted Bungee

Son of Spam

The Night Talker

Jeffrey Embalmer

The Handsome Family

Hannibal Lecture

The Golden State Filler, DDS

Orgies and Sex Clubs

They're more awkward than you think!

Viva Las Vegas!

Have you checked out the latest casinos yet?

Atlantis

The waiters wear only codpieces in this salt-water **Sodom** catering to real whales. Get in the buffet line early for the **steamed lobsters**; they get crabby by the end of their shift.

Stalag 21

The anorexic male servers have shaved heads and wear striped prison suits. The **hardtack** and **gruel** are to die for. High rollers who can't pay off their debts are **shot before sunrise** for the late crowd.

Robo World

A budgeter's delight. Tip the squeaky-clean card dealers with **WD-40**.

The French Revolution

Lifelike guillotines cut the cards and anyone **caught cheating**.

Hades

No air-conditioning. **No fire exits**. And the staff are real demons. **Helpful hint:** Don't call room service!

The Asylum

Looks just like a mental hospital. The commissary serves **cold food** and uses only **plastic forks** and knives. Since the card dealers are schizophrenic, you have to **beat them twice** to win.

The Twilight Zone

Win a jackpot on every spin. Blackjack dealers always bust. The **pit bosses** are visually **impaired seniors**. The spooky theme song runs on an endless loop. Cover charge is $500 to get in, **$1,000 to get out.**

50
Shades of Sequels

Spin-offs that got tied up in production:

50 Shades of Hay
All bets and bridles are off as a stable of stallions sow their **wild oats** in this barnyard thriller. Stars **Mr. Ed**.

50 Shades of Greyhounds
Watch the sparks, fleas and 101 Dalmatians fly in a **kinky kennel**. With fetching cameos by Lady and the Tramp, this **campy romp** already has **Lassie** smelling **Oscar**.

50 Shades of Glade
The **hijinks** begin when our heroes discover they both have highly sensitive **erogenous zones** deep inside their nostrils.

50 Shades of Shades
Well-heeled nudists wearing only Ray-Bans cavort at a **midnight masquerade** party in this **raw nail-biter**. Spot-on soundtrack by **Corey Hart**.

50 Shades of Gravy
Cranberries and mashed potatoes will never look the same after this **steamy docudrama**.

WHAT IF Classic Rock Had to Be
POLiTiCALLY CORRECT?

Classics from yesteryear that would never get past the PC Police today:

Cat Scratch Fever
by Ted Nugent
Just for being by Ted Nugent.

Walk on the Wild Side
by Lou Reed
The chorus should've been,
"And the African-American women of color go …"!

A Boy Named Sue
by Johnny Cash
Why couldn't the song have ended with a shout-out to "Memo, Jorge … Any nombre pero Susana?"

99 Problems
by Jay-Z
Don't we have enough problems already?

Smoke on the Water
by Deep Purple
How lame. Couldn't they find a vape?

Pretty Woman
by Roy Orbison
Change title and lyrics to
"Pretty Person (Walking Down the Street)"

White Rabbit
by Jefferson Airplane
Call PETA!

White Wedding
by Billy Idol
Seriously?

I Saw Her Standing There
by The Beatles
Pronoun problem! Change the lyrics to
"I Saw Her/Him/Them/Standing/Sitting/
Lying/Chilling/Twerking There."

Born in the USA
by Bruce Springsteen
But are you 'woke?

Hotel California
by The Eagles
Closed until further notice.

A SHORT HISTORY OF DISCO

FEBRUARY 1977
Saturday Night Fever opens in theaters across America.

JULY 1977
Saturday Night Fever soundtrack hits the
$20 million in sales mark.

DECEMBER 1977
The term Disco Sucks is coined by an LA radio station.

AUGUST 1978
A Philadelphia radio station sponsors the first
Stamp Out Disco bonfire.

JANUARY 1980
The Disco Liberation Army forms in Berkeley.

MARCH 1980
Governor Brown takes his Stamp Out Disco message
to the Democratic Primary in New Hampshire.
He's routed by a not-yet-outed John Travolta.

JULY 1980
Presidential hopeful **Jimmy Carter** promises to deport the **Bee Gees** if he's elected.

AUGUST 1980
Donna Summer falls in love with her captors after she's kidnapped by the **Disco Liberation Army**.

SEPTEMBER 1980
Donna Summer and the **Disco Liberation Army** jump the line and rob **Studio 54** in broad strobe-light.

OCTOBER 1980
Polyester-clad protestors converge on the nation's capital singing, **All we are saying is, teach us to dance.**

DECEMBER 1980
Disco disappears everywhere except in a few gay bars.

JANUARY 1984
Just as **George Orwell** predicted, a singer named **Madonna** brings disco back to the mainstream with her hit single, **Like a Vegan.**

~ Originally published in
Santa Cruz Good Times
on March 27, 1980
Updated in July 2020 to make
me look like Nostradamus
*(A Polish Death Metal band,
not the fortune teller)*

PART 4

MY
Appendix
HURTS

First up in my sore Appendix is a yarn by
Calamity Jane.

Discretion is advised
due to Calamity's **explicit descriptions**
of frontier life in Chico.

Calamity Jane
and the Hooker Oak

A good friend of mine whose name I can't
remember found this hastily scrawled **message
in a bottle** under the old **Hooker Oak** tree
when it was toppled by a storm in 1977:

I don't reckon but that only a few of the **young'uns**
roamin' these parts nowadays will've ever know'd
how this here **giant oak tree** up and got its name.
I further reckon it's high time ya'll learned.

Maybe you already heard-tell how I **hightailed it** outa
Deadwood after that feller snuck up on my beloved
Wild Bill. He was the prettiest man I ever did see, Wild
Bill wuz. **Hell's bells** but did that **gunslinger** know
how to ride bareback. Why'z, I reckon he'd be itchin'
for another hitchin' right now, **poker face** and all, if
he hadn't up and got hisself dealt such a **bad hand**.

Ol' Deadwood did Wild Bill
proud with that **wingdinger**
of a funeral, though.
I out-drunk everyone there
'cept'n maybe **Doc Holliday**.
Then I purt-near didn't stop
a cussin' and cursin' till the
Wichita-Pacific Surfliner
dropped me off in
Sacratomato not but a **hard
day's night** or two later.

ED AGE 1000 YEARS. BIDWELL PARK, CHICO, CALIFORNIA

Some **party gals** from **Gridley** hitched aboard the Stagecoach we wuz ridin' some 30 miles outside that new fangled stretch of waterin' holes along the **Esplanade** in **Chico**. We wuz all drinkin' whiskey and **laudanum** and **what-not** till two of the gals fell asleep on my lap.

Far as I know, those **gussied-up gold diggaz** never did wake up neither. I just plain lost track after the handsome young sheriff stopped by to **'vestigate**. He didn't have a clue nor care much to look for one with the drapes shut nice-n tight like they wuz and jes me 'n him there bumpin' along at **High Noon** with them pretty gals snorin' away next to us. His britches were hunkered down 'roun' his boots and mine's was off altogether when the poor feller **plum lost his six-shooter**. Loaded with nothing but blanks, turns out. We'z two wuz a sight, all right. Next thing, the livery pulled up to the **Bidwell** homestead. There she was, sittin' pretty as a postcard. My Lord, but didn't that precious **Annie** look fine enough to nibble like a crumpet as she curtsied our arrival.

I woulda been tickled as a **plump pig** to spend the rest of my born days carin' for Miss Annie and those **beautiful curls** of hers. Why, they wuz almost as nice to touch and twirl as Wild Bill's, they wuz. Lo and behold, jes when Annie and me and her honey badger husband, the ol' **General Bidwell** hisself, well, all three of us wuz gettin' plastered proper-like in the parlor, when Big John up and remembers he's a **gen-u-wine teetotaler.**

A **fool-on Proheebitionist**, matter a fact. Said my lack of 'ligious morals was to blame for all the prior 'citement down in Dixie. Meanin' south of his gentleman's vest. The Gen'l wuz none too pleased neither to learn the two gals from **Gridley** got **way-laid** afore they could even set their dainty feet down in the private crick he has **beaver dammed** out back.

After all the fuss died down, Miss Annie and I both had a **good romp** in the hay with the stable boy afore the General started gettin' 'spicious again. When he caught me all gussied up in petticoats with Annie tom-foolerin' around in a **harness, holster** and **handcuffs**, why my goose was cooked.

'Twas delicious, too, with the gravy and dumplin's Miss Annie had the servants whup up.

After supper, the Gen'l says I best pack my bags and catch the next stage outa Durham if'n I wasn't lookin' to sport a real bad **neckburn**. Said there was a good **hangin' tree** just wait'n for me; said he wuz determined to name it in my honor on account of all the **commotion** and sinnin' I'd caused since my arrival at **Bidwell Manor**.

Bless her sweet soul, Annie slipped me a bottle of fine **local whiskey** just as I was fixin' to get on the stagecoach. This fine likker was de'stilled in **Hell Town**, the label said. But, hell's bells, if'n it didn't taste like **Paradise** to me.

Turns out the handsum feller steerin' our horse and buggy was **powerful thirsty**, too. Why, I reckon he'll be joinin' me back here in the coach soon's he's finished diggin' a hole for this here **whiskey** bottle. I plan to bury it there with this note soon's we'z done **playin' hankypanky** on the fine hanky I found in the **Gen'l's drawers**.

The handsome livery boy Ben says the constable don't take kindly to folks **buggerin'** all over creation and such with an **open container** in the coach. And why, don't this beat all! The **giant oak tree** shadin' us from the good Lord's pryin' eyes 'aint but the same tree Gen'l Bidwell promised to **hang me from**. Or at least name after me, if I didn't mind my **Pees** and **Qs**.

Well, I'm **fierce determined** these fine hickeys will be the only marks left on my **purty neck** after I **blow this town**. So I jes' hope and prays that whatever name Gen'l Bidwell goes and gives to this old oak tree will do me proud!

In closin', on account of my needin' to **hightail** it back to **Deadwood**, here's a warm smack on the hiney to the lucky devil who finds this **Message in a Bottle** someday. I jes' hope it ain't **The Police**! Be a honey bear would-ya and make sure it gits printed in one of them **fancy books** I sees the higher classes totin' aroun' on their travels.

Eternally yours,

Calamity Jane

Miss Calamity Jane

The Life & Death
of the Party

Remember the Hippies?

They were the generation that
rioted against **The War**, rioted for **Civil Rights**,
rioted for **Free Speech** and complained
because their parents didn't like their **Beatle haircuts**.

They **smoked pot, dropped acid** and
invented the catch-phrase
"Never Trust Anyone Over 30."

If ever there were a generation that was going to stay
young at heart, you'd think this was **Them**.
Instead, the first wave of **baby boomers** is
already as **rigid** and **frigid** as their parents ever were.

Maybe more so.

They hate new bands like the **Clash**
more than their parents hated **Mick Jagger**.
They've changed "Never Trust Anyone Over 30"
to "Shut Up If You're Under 25."

And their kids, if they have any,
aren't even out of their **Pampers** yet.

I took a few **albums** to a party
last week. Most of the people there
were in their late 20s or early 30s.
Ex-hippies. English majors. Philosophy
professors. **Liberal**. Open-minded.

Or so I thought.

Midway through the
party, I made the mistake
of mentioning I'd brought
the new **Sex Pistols'** album.
It was like I'd just shouted
a dirty word in church.
Someone wanted to wash *my* mouth out
with **Tom's of Maine** tooth paste.
Others suggested hanging.

The professor of **medieval history** wanted
to draw and quarter me.
In a jumping jack flash, I went from the life of the party to
an outcast. The hostess, a veteran of the
Berkeley Free Speech Movement, asked me to not
ever mention the **Sex Pistols** again.

I learned an important lesson that night.
You can talk about **Karl Marx** at a college mixer.
You can talk about the **Beatles**,
Gestalt therapy, **organic gardening**
and **premature ejaculation** if you
make it quick.
But don't bring up new bands like
the Sex Pistols around **aging hippies** unless
you're prepared to **get punked**.

~ Originally published in the **Butte County Bugle**
on February 9, 1978

RADICAL
Chic

Susan Shelby, the charming host
of the featured party, was furious at me
when she first saw the **Sex Pistols** article.
Within a few days, she'd changed her tune.

Turned out it wasn't such a bad thing, socially,
for her **shindig** to have been memorialized
in print for the whole town to read.

Meanwhile, I felt like **Tom Wolfe** writing for
New York Magazine about
cocktail socialists on **Park Avenue**.

R.I.P.
HOOKER OAK
1652-1977

CONFESSIONS
of a
Parsley Grower

Local cops say over 100 counter-culture scofflaws grow parsley for a living in the secret **spice fields** of the **Sierra Nevada** foothills. One of these intrepid farmers, Winston T. Fabreze of 103 Cohasset Stage, gave me his full name and address after I promised not to tell anyone.

So, Winston, how'd you get started in this racket?
I grew my first crops in a closet in The Haight during the **peace-love-parsley-power** days. When that scene fizzled out, I moved north and became the **hip** capitalist you see today.

How much money have you made over the years?
Well, the first year I got busted. Then, we got **ripped off** by rednecks. Two years ago, **Bigfoot** caught me with my pants down. I'm still pretty sore about that. Last year, the trimmers **got stoned** and burned up our fall harvest in the microwave. So, altogether, I've made at least **five dollars and 67 cents**. Less after health, dental and fire insurance for the trimmers!

How big do parsley plants get these days?
Humongous, brah. Some of the females are over four inches tall already.

How much is parsley going for on the black market?
We're getting anywhere from 15 to 35 cents a sprig now,
depending on the strain and quality. More for heirloom.

Any favorite strains?
My new Cohasset Chronic is catching
fire with the Hollywood set. I'm also
working on a **gnarly catnip and
parsley hybrid** with hints of **cumin** and
oregano. Just to add a little spice.

Achoooooo! Rip-offs still a problem?
Not since I released a litter of attack-
trained **Dobermans** on the property.
They were rescues, by the way.
Neutered, too. So, they're always
pissed. The electric fence, land mines
and **howitzers** also help keep out **looky-loos**. The key
is to avoid suspicion or attracting any attention.

Where are your plants located anyway?
Oh, well. They're really easy to get to. Just head up
Cohasset Highway till you get to the little antique shop.
Then hang a right and tramp through the **poison oak**
till you see the **Dobermans** coming at you. You're not
writing any of this stuff down are you?

**Nah. Trust me, brah. Any
tips for my readers?**
Remember to feed
the Dobermans. And,
whatever you do, don't
tell **anyone** where your
plants are located!

- *Butte County Bugle*
November 16, 1978

Here was my first stab
at a movie review!

A Little **Blood** on the **Popcorn,** Please

Midnight. Saturday.

The El Rey Theater was packed with foot-stomping maniacs. The lights dimmed, the curtains parted, and the words **The Texas Chainsaw Massacre** appeared on the screen in blood-red letters.

The crowd **roared**. Like the Rolling Stones had just stepped on stage. As the opening credits roll, the cheers grow **louder**. The more gruesome the photo the louder the cheers.

Wow.

This was unsettling. It was okay to watch **horror** movies in quiet terror. But you don't go and cheer at the **blood and guts**.

At least I thought you didn't.

Those cheering loudest looked like normal students, like you'd see in class or the **library**. Now they were screaming for more **blood**.

"All right!"

someone behind me yelled as the onscreen carnage continued.

"Get down!"

screamed another.

I slunk into my seat and tried to hide in my hoodie. As the first **idiot** walks up to a spooky-looking farmhouse, you know **something terrible** is going to happen. He opens the screen door and looks inside.

"Go for it, sucker!"
someone screamed.

The **numbskull** in the movie inches down the hall toward a wall hung with **animal skins** and **skulls**. I peeked down the row I was seated in and saw a woman being **strangled** by a man in the seat behind her. I jumped up to help her, but everyone **yelled** for me to sit back down. So I went back to my seat and watched helplessly until she stopped kicking.

"KILL, KILL, KILL, KILL, KILL!"
chanted the crowd.

Each murder gets gorier.

In the end, the chainsaw killer chases the last vacationer for **20 minutes** through dense underbrush and **finally** out to a highway, where she's **rescued** by a kindly truck driver.

Bummer.

After the movie, I hurried into the street
to beat the **mob**. Some of the more **impressionable**
viewers had broken into Collier's Hardware,
looted the store of its **chainsaws**, and were now
terrorizing pedestrians on the sidewalk.
I saw a man chase down a **young kid** and
saw him in half in front of the funeral home
across from the SBX.

As I rushed to make my **deadline**, I heard the
roar of a **thousand chainsaws** over the telltale beating of
my heart under a **blood-red Chico State pullover.**

~ Originally published in the
Chico News and Review
on March 31, 1977

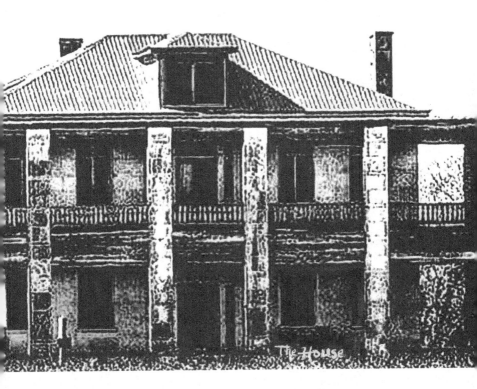

A Headline
that was
Off the Chain (saw)

The chainsaw piece caused quite a buzz around town. Credit for the great headline goes to **Robert Speer**, then editor of the Chico News and Review.

Like a freak without warning, I dropped the Chainsaw piece off at Speer's office on a Tuesday night. And there it was, surprise twist and all, to be read or shred by 15,000 students on Thursday.

"A little blood on the popcorn, please."

I had people quoting that line back to me for weeks.

Robert Speer was great at recognizing a complete lack of talent when he saw it and always printing my stuff anyway. Even though I wrote mainly for the throwaway across town.

Remember those Silly, Sappy

Trash Singles
of
Yesteryear?

Slap yourself silly if you don't know most of these answers.
Kick **your own ass** if you miss them all!

1. In the song *867-5309/Jenny*, where did the horny singer get Jenny's phone number?

    a. from Stacy's mom
    b. from Rick Springfield's Little Red Book
    c. from a bathroom wall

2. What got **run over** in Louden Wainwright's only hit?

    a. La Cucaracha
    b. A Skunk
    c. A Horse with No Name
    d. A Horse Named Wildfire

3. Who sang *Louie, Louie*?

    a. Louis Armstrong
    b. Chubby Checker
    c. Modern Talking
    d. The Kingsmen
    e. Stories
    f. Hot Chocolate

4. *Who Let the **Dogs** Out?*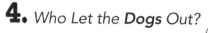
- **a.** Snoop Dogg
- **b.** The Pussycat Dolls
- **c.** Baha Men
- **d.** Vanilla Ice

5. Phil Spector is best known for:
- **a.** being a **weirdo**
- **b.** murder
- **c.** his **love of guns**
- **d.** wall of sound production technique
- **e.** all of the above

6. What comes right after the word '**Whoomp**' in Tag Team's only and most annoying hit?
- **a.** 'Your ass'
- **b.** 'There it is!'
- **c.** 'Where'd it go?'
- **d.** 'Shoop'
- **e.** 'Whoop-de-do'

7. What was the name of **The Detergents**' only hit?
- **a.** *Little Honda*
- **b.** *The Little Old Lady from Pasadena*
- **c.** *Leader of the Pack*
- **d.** *Ring Around the Collar*
- **e.** *Leader of the Laundromat*

8. Who sang about those lovely '**lady lumps**' in the irritating club classic *My Humps*?

a. The Trumps
b. The Bumps
c. Salt-N-Pepa
d. Black Eyed Peas
e. Black Eyed Susan
f. Hanson

9. Someone left **what** out in the rain in *MacArthur Park*?

a. the laundry
b. a cheesecake
c. a key lime pie
d. a cake with green icing
e. green eggs and ham
f. Marie Callender

10. Whose biggest-selling album was aptly titled *Trash*?

a. Ratt
b. Rancid
c. Hoobastank
d. Garbage
e. Meat Loaf
f. Alice Cooper

⭐ **Bonus Question:**

Who jumped off the **Tallahatchee Bridge**?

a. The Harper Valley PTA
b. Billy Joe MacAllister
c. Richard Cory

1. c. The **bathroom wall**. I'm still trying to reach Jessie's Girl and Stacy's Mom.

2. b. Louden Wainwright's magnus opus, *Dead Skunk in the Middle of the Road*, stank all the way up to #16 in 1972.

3. d. The groups Hot Chocolate, Modern Talking and Stories all hit the charts with *Brother Louie*. But it was **The Kingsmen** who rocked *Louie, Louie*.

4. c. Unfortunately, the Bahamian roots reggae band **Baha Men** let the dogs out.

5. e. **All of the above** define **Phil Spector**. RIP. Not.

6. b. '*Whoomp. There it* (was)!' Count yourself lucky if you missed this one.

7. e. **The Detergents** quickly dissolved after this sudsy parody of the Shangrilas' hit, *Leader of the Pack*.

8. d. **Black Eyed Peas** took their lumps for this one.

9. **d.** All that endless caterwauling over a **green cake** melting in the rain? Yuck. I'll take In-A-Gadda-Da-Vida.

10. **e. Alice Cooper** struck multi-platinum 'Poison' with this last blast of 80s hair metal.

Bonus Answer: b. Billy Joe MacAllister.
Two decades before Green Day!

SCORING

7-11 correct: Smart (ass)! Have you gotten your annual prostate exam yet this year? I have.

3-6 correct: Not bad. But why are you looking to me for approval? Gosh darnit, you'll be just fine.

1-2 correct: Duh. Of course, you know Jenny's number by heart and all about those lady lumps!

0 correct: Stick to the movie quizzes.

What Your Score Says About You

That you had some spare time on your hands.

Thank you for wasting it with me!

~ An abridged version of my original article, which appeared in the *SF Chronicle* on July 13, 1980

Poorly Timed
COMMERCIAL
BREAKS

These are some ridiculous commercial breaks
I've seen or **imagined seeing** over the years:

President Bill Clinton doing the deed in a TV movie
about **Monica Lewinsky** ...
to an ad for Oxi-Clean Spot Remover.

Steven Weed getting his ass
kicked by the SLA in
The Ordeal of Patty Hearst ...
to a Weed-Eater whacking
away at full throttle.

Clint Eastwood as the
innocent victim of a
lynch mob in
Hang 'em High ...
to a nifty jingle for Ring Around the Collar!

Cat Woman in black leather tights
and **'do-me-right-now'** boots
as she starts to kiss Batman ...
to a mouth-watering message from the makers of
Puss-n-Boots cat chow.

Planet of the Apes ...
to the Geico Caveman.

In **Roots**, the escaped slave Kunta Kinte
surrounded by vicious attack dogs ...
to a Golden Retriever slobbering over its master in a
Gravy Train commercial.

Joan of Arc trembling at
the stake ... to fast-lighting
**Kingston Charcoal
Briquettes**.

Sir Thomas More waiting
for the axe ...
to New & Improved
Head and Shoulders
anti-dandruff shampoo.

The **Ned Beatty** character
squealing like a pig in **Deliverance** ...
to an ad for **Preparation H**.

~ Abridged and updated from my original article
in the *San Francisco Chronicle*
on September 18, 1979

So You Want a
CIVIL WAR...

Civil War might seem like a blast to the old-timers who reenact the **Battle of Gettysburg** every year. But they're no picnic, folks. Just ask Abe Lincoln.

Consider the sporting ramifications, just for starters. NFL fans are split pretty much 50% **Democrats**, 50% **Republicans** and 50% neither of the above.

Let me ask all you SF 49er fans a simple question: If you met a fellow gold-digger wearing a **MAGA cap** and drinking Anchor Steam on tap, would you rather raise a toast to **Joe Montana, Dwight Clark** and **The Catch,** or assault your new buddy with a pickaxe and shovel?

Looking to the hundreds of New York Jets fans who want **Biden** to start over **Trump** at quarterback. Reminisce with a Trump supporter about **Broadway Joe** or discuss the finer points of **hair fragrance** with **Baltimore Joe**?

Music? Think of all the cold beer and margaritas that would be spilled, and maybe lost forever, by brawling Jimmy Buffet factions in a **Battle of the Parrot Heads**.

There are fashion considerations as well.
The **Democrats** will likely fare fine in whatever chic ensemble of blue they choose. But, seriously, will the **Republican** militias feel comfortable wearing **Red Coats**?

Baseball? Think fast:
Mike Trout or **Jefferson Davis** as your center fielder?

Black Friday at Wal-Mart? The **Red State Rednecks** would be VERY heavy favorites here. But don't count out the lean and mean **Blue-City Brawlers** when push comes to shove in this holiday matchup.

On Halloween, do we really want our kids saying **"Trump or Treat?"**

McDonald's.
"Caution: The **Unhappy Happy Meal customer** behind you may be armed and dangerous."

Neighborhood barbecues and potlucks?
Once the street battles begin, this All-American pastime will be strictly **BYOGAAA** ("Bring Your Own Guns, Ammo and Arsenic").

Church groups: "As a friendly reminder,
Thou Shall Not Kill Thy Neighbor or Thy Fellow Parishioner, Please."

Office politics. Do your colleagues bleed **blue** or **red**? You'll soon find out! Paintball as team-building? Not on your life.

Going to a nightclub? If the deejay's playing hip-hop, house, trance or Woody Guthrie, chances are you'll be coming (or going) down with the **Blues**.

Line dancers? Best not shake your **Buttigieg!**

Interested in taking someone home for a nightcap? Just don't chit-chat over a Marlboro afterwards.

Finally, is your **neighborhood drug supplier** a lib or a con? Likely an **EX-con**, but who's taking chances?

I'll conclude today's broadside with two more broadsides:

Maybe we Americans have more in common than we think.

And could you pass the apple pie, please?

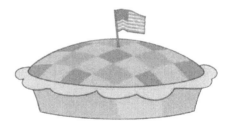

SOME Hella Expressions

Everyone from **SoCal** adds "The" before describing any freeway or highway interchange.
As in:
"Just take The 101 to The 405 to The 5 to The 55 to The 91 and keep going past The Barstow till you drive straight off The Pier in The Atlantic City."

Anyone who says Hella is from **NoCal**. Unless her name is **Gwen Stefani**.

In **Chico**, students and townspeople alike knock the 'L' out of random words like '**almond**.' Who knows why in the 'L' they do this.

In **Santa Cruz**, any female over the age of one minute must be referred to as a 'woman.' As in, 'This young woman has a diaper rash and needs to burp.' This law would have really screwed up the collected works of **Joe Francis**, **Motley Crue** and the **Beatles**.

In **Monterey**, locals have two technical terms for the weather: **Foggy** and **foggier**.

Denizens of Orange County beach towns like **Costa Mesa** and **Newport Beach** must always know, 24/7/365, how big the waves are pumping at **The Wedge**.

In **Sonoma**, one quickly learns to appreciate the '**nose**' or finely blended aroma of **cabernet** and **cannabis**.

'Not for nothing' is the state motto of **New Jersey** 'not for nothing.'

You can win bar bets with this **knowledge**!

We Can Work It Out

Life is very short,
and there's no t-i-i-i-m-e,
for fussing and fighting, my friend.
So, I will ask you once again
to shut up and see it my way.

**Luckily for you,
this will all be over soon.**

And you won't remember a thing.

The Cradle will ROCK

My Father, 40 Years Ago

"Why in the hell would anyone brag about their college being the #1 Party School in the Nation?"

Me, 40 Years Later

"Because we had some Hella Good Times between The 5 and The 99, Dad. We Had Some Hella Good Times."

This week's profile ... C L Smith

We caught up with the spirited Chico State booster and worst-selling author to talk trash on a recent Zoom call. Thankfully, this interview was conducted from the waist up:

What's on your bookstand right now?

An original iPad with the screen stuck on the **Porn Hub** landing page. Say, you wouldn't happen to know any **horny hackers** who make house calls, would you?

Describe your ideal reading experience.

Relaxing on a private jet over Monaco with a bevy of **supermodels** attending to my every need is always nice. But I'll settle for the rear window of a non-stop commercial **flight to Paris** if I can get the whole row, an open bar and **Mr. Pillow**. Also, an iPad and my favorite blankie!

What's your favorite book no one else has heard of?

Tongue in Chico by C L Smith. It's a stunningly stupid work by a deservedly unknown author, but one who could use a little fun money to spend on **private jets** and **supermodels**.

What book should everyone read before the age of 10?
The Iliad by Homer, of course. On parchment. In Latin and the original Greek. Then you should memorize the **German, French** and **Swahili** translations of **Beowolf**. Like, duh, now! But isn't that what everyone recommends?

What's the best book you've ever received as a gift?
The World According to Garp with a vial of **primo baby laxative** tucked into a cut-out stash space in the middle.

What famous book was overrated?
The World According to Garp. Because there was a huge **hole** in the plot, and it made me **have to go** to the bathroom really bad.

Which fiction writers working today do you admire?
Sean Hannity is an amazing storyteller. Another **up-and-comer** to look out for is Endall Beall, the Q-Anon guy. These are two of the most **brilliant satirists** out there. Affectionate **pen pals**, too, from what I hear.

What kind of reader were you as a child?
The kind who read mainly **Hardy Boy** books till I was 12 and ruined every **Playboy** magazine I could get my hands on between the ages of 13 and 20.

You're organizing a literary dinner party. Which writers, living or deceased, do you invite?
Jenna Jameson in her prime. Monica Lewinsky, to discuss the alternate use of **fine cigars.** Emily Dickinson for the **swimsuit-optional** after-party. And Mark Twain but not Sam Clemens. Because Mark Twain was way more fun!

After**word**

Word.

I've always wanted to do that!

For the purposes of this history,
I've treated the era from 1980 to the present
like a **Russian textbook**
and omitted any disturbing things
that might have happened in
the world after
The Rocky Horror Picture Show
and **Texas Chainsaw Massacre**.
If this book sells, look for the sequel,
Tongue in Chico 2,
coming as soon as I write it
to wherever fine books aren't sold.

(It's hard saying good-bye.)

Acknowledgements

Debonair Mad Man David Bowen was the creative mastermind of the CYHMN campaign for Verizon. OG Googler Jonathan Matus was the one-man army behind the Android launch. Richard Peifer, you rock for having the Balls Beyond Walls to publish my column for three years in The Bugle.

Thank you to my siblings Spencer, Lawson and Louise for LTFAO over the first draft; to my brother Graham for inspiring me to write this book in the first place; to Muriel Garcia for the early props; to Shyann Tryber for the 55 wpm; to Randy Hensley, Tom Reck and Joel and Rose-Ellen Leonard for the good times in Chico; to Jay Shore and Melody Quarnstrom for the lessons in publishing; to Brian Jones, Mike Benvenuti, Bill Bettencourt, Brian Shay, Mike Finley, Rob Miller, Joe Saracino, John Harrobin, Marni Walden and Tami Erwin for the career assists in wireless; to David Rotenberg, Tom Long and Julie Morrow for the smart edits to this book; to Bruce Barta for the laughs of a lifetime; to David Berger, Jack Fisher and Allen Harthorn for the Chico cred; to James Pendergast for the expert proofreading; to Tierney Smith for the wicked web design; to Kevin and Autumn Croninfor the pen name and witty blurbs; to Randy Nowell for bringing the book to life with your amazing art; and to my lovely wife Nancy for the back rubs.

Index

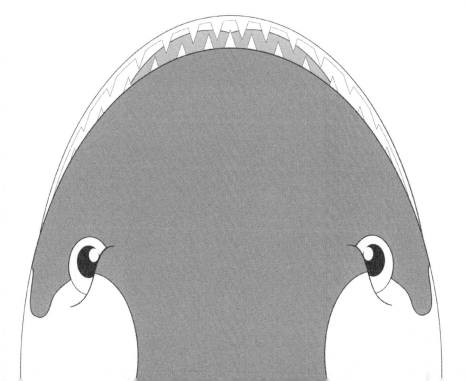

Made in the USA
Monee, IL
09 June 2021